QUICK & EASY COOKING

PARRAGON

QUICK & EASY
COOKING

Photography by Peter Barry
Designed by Richard Hawke and Claire Leighton
Edited by Jillian Stewart and Kate Cranshaw
Recipes by Judith Ferguson, Lalita Ahmed and Carolyn Garner

3449

This edition published in 1993 by Coombe Books
for Parragon Book Service Ltd.,
707 High Road, Finchley, London N12 0BT

Printed in Hong Kong
ISBN 1-85813-371-8

Contents

Introduction

Many people who do not have much time and energy to spend shopping or preparing meals have resorted to buying 'fast food' in the form of ready-prepared meals and take-aways. Unfortunately, as well as being an expensive way to eat, it does not necessarily guarantee an adequate supply of vitamins, minerals and fibre. For these very reasons, there has been something of a resurgence of home-cooking with an emphasis on quick and easy meals. With this in mind it is essential to know how to prepare food quickly and, just as importantly, what ingredients to use for the minimum of effort. Certain foods such as pasta, salads, fish, shellfish and eggs, are perfectly suited to quick cooking, but it is often the choice of meat which people find difficult. The various cuts best suited to quick cooking are as follows:

Beef - steak and minute steak, mince
Veal - escalopes, calves' liver
Pork - tenderloin (sliced into medallions), mince, steaks, chops, escalopes, liver
Lamb - noisettes, cutlets, leg chops, neck fillet, liver, kidney
Poultry - breast, escalopes, mince, liver
Game - duck breast, venison steak

Obviously, the method of cooking is all important, and you will find that in *Quick and Easy Cooking* there is less baking in the oven and more grilling, pan- and stir-frying and sautéeing. These short methods of cooking are very effective with the cuts of meat and fish already mentioned. Organisation and making the most of the time that you have available is all important. For cooks in a hurry the freezer can be most advantageous, as many people find it easier to do a large amount of cooking when they have the time, freeze it, and buy accompaniments such as fresh fruit and vegetables as required.

When short of time, entertaining can pose a problem. Planning is the key to success here and ease of preparation paramount. Choose one or two dishes, such as a starter (try Quick Liver Paté, Fennel and Orange Croustade or Stuffed Eggs) and a dessert, (such as Crepes, Strawberry Cloud, or Chocolate Brandy Mousse) that can be prepared in advance, even the day before. Dishes that can be part prepared and then frozen are also a boon, but remember to allow sufficient thawing time in your schedule. The main course should be something easy but effective, such as Trout with Chive Sauce, Chicken with Cherries, or Veal Scallopine with Prosciutto. This allows you the maximum time with guests, with the minimum of fuss and effort.

As you can see, successful quick and easy cooking may require a bit of thought at first and perhaps some change to your normal cooking style, but once undertaken this new way of cooking will soon become second nature and the term 'fast food' will have a new meaning in your household.

SPINACH AND APPLE SOUP

The two main flavours complement each other perfectly in this hearty soup.

SERVES 4

30g/1oz butter or margarine
1 small onion, chopped
30g/1oz flour
570ml/1 pint vegetable stock
450g/1lb spinach, shredded
225g/8oz apple purée
280ml/½ pint milk
Salt and freshly ground black pepper
Pinch of nutmeg
Lemon juice
Natural yogurt
A little parsley, finely chopped

1. Melt the butter in a large saucepan and sauté the onion until soft.

2. Add the flour and cook to a pale straw colour.

3. Add the stock slowly, stirring well, and simmer for 10 minutes.

4. Add the spinach and cook until tender.

5. Cool slightly and mix in the apple purée.

6. Place all the ingredients in a liquidiser and blend until smooth.

7. Return to the pan and reheat slowly together with the milk.

8. Add the salt and pepper, nutmeg and lemon juice to taste.

9. Serve in individual bowls with the yogurt swirled on the top and garnished with chopped parsley.

TIME: Preparation takes 15 minutes, cooking takes 15 minutes.

COOK'S TIP: The apple purée can be omitted if not available but it adds an unusual flavour to the soup.

VARIATIONS: If there is no vegetable water available for the stock, a stock cube can be mixed with 570ml/1 pint of boiling water instead.

EASY LENTIL SOUP

A good old-fashioned soup which is sure to please all the family.

SERVES 4-6

225g/8oz split red lentils
30g/1oz butter or margarine
1 medium onion, finely chopped
2 celery stalks, finely diced
2 carrots, finely diced
Grated rind of 1 lemon
1150ml/2 pints light vegetable stock
Salt and freshly ground black pepper

1. Pick over the lentils and remove any stones. Rinse well.

2. Heat the butter or margarine in a pan and sauté the onion for 2-3 minutes.

3. Add the diced celery and carrots and let the vegetables sweat for 5-10 minutes.

4. Stir in the lentils, add the lemon rind, stock and salt and pepper to taste.

5. Bring to the boil, reduce the heat and simmer for 15-20 minutes until the vegetables are tender.

6. Roughly blend the soup in a liquidiser; it should not be too smooth.

7. Check the seasoning and reheat gently.

TIME: Preparation takes about 10 minutes, cooking takes 15-20 minutes.

SERVING IDEAS: Sprinkle with cheese and serve with hot toast.

TO FREEZE: Freeze for up to 3 months.

Prawn Soup

A hearty soup that makes a meal accompanied by some crusty bread.

SERVES 6

45g/1½oz butter or margarine
1 onion, finely chopped
1 red pepper, finely chopped
2 celery sticks, finely chopped
1 clove garlic, crushed
Pinch dry mustard
2 tsps paprika
3 tbsps flour
1150ml/2 pints fish stock
1 sprig thyme and 1 bay leaf
225g/8oz raw, peeled prawns
Salt and pepper
Snipped chives

1. Melt the butter or margarine and add the onion, pepper, celery and garlic. Cook gently to soften.

2. Stir in the mustard, paprika and flour. Cook for about 3 minutes over gentle heat, stirring occasionally.

3. Pour on the stock gradually, stirring until well blended. Add the thyme and bay leaf and bring to the boil. Reduce the heat and simmer about 5 minutes or until thickened, stirring occasionally.

4. Add the prawns and cook until pink and curled – about 5 minutes. Season with salt and pepper to taste and top with snipped chives before serving.

TIME: Preparation takes about 15 minutes and cooking takes about 8-10 minutes.

VARIATIONS: If using peeled, cooked prawns add just before serving and heat through for about 2 minutes only.

COOK'S TIP: Cook spices such as paprika briefly before adding any liquid to develop their flavour and eliminate any harsh taste.

Miso Soup

This delicious soup of Japanese origin makes a nice change for a starter.

SERVES 2

1 small onion, grated
2cm/¾-inch fresh root ginger, peeled and finely chopped
1 clove garlic, crushed
1 tbsp sesame oil
1 carrot, finely sliced
¼ small cauliflower, divided into florets
1150ml/2 pints water
1 large tbsp arame (Japanese seaweed)
30g/1oz peas (fresh or frozen)
2 tbsps shoyu (Japanese soy sauce)
1 tbsp miso (soya bean paste)
Black pepper to taste
2 spring onions, finely chopped

1. Sauté the onion, ginger and garlic in the sesame oil for a few minutes.

2. Add the carrot and cauliflower and gently sweat the vegetables for 5 minutes.

3. Add the water, arame, peas and shoyu. Cook for 15-20 minutes or until the vegetables are soft.

4. Blend the miso to a paste with a little of the soup liquid and add to the soup, but do not allow to boil.

5. Season with freshly ground black pepper to taste.

6. Serve garnished with chopped spring onions.

TIME: Preparation takes 15 minutes, cooking takes 20 minutes.

SERVING IDEAS: Serve with hot garlic bread.

VARIATIONS: Substitute other vegetables such as mooli, turnip, swede, mange tout or green beans, but remember that this soup is mainly a broth with a few floating vegetables.

COOK'S TIP: Arame, shoyu and miso are available from Japanese grocers and some health food specialists.

Crouton Studded Crispy Prawn Balls

These crispy, crouton coated prawn balls make an excellent starter or snack.

SERVES 4

4 slices white bread
225g/8oz white fish fillets
225g/8oz shelled prawns
2 tsps salt
Pepper to taste
2 egg whites
2 slices fresh root ginger
2 tbsp cornflour
Oil for deep frying

1. Remove crusts from the bread. Cut each slice into small crouton-sized cubes. Spread out on a large baking tray and dry in a hot oven until slightly browned.

2. Chop the fish and prawns very finely. Mix together with the salt, pepper, egg white, finely chopped ginger, and cornflour. Blend well.

3. Shape the mixture into 5cm/2-inch balls, and roll over the croutons to coat.

4. Heat the oil in a deep fryer. Add the crouton studded prawn balls one by one. Turn with a perforated spoon until evenly browned, this takes about 2 minutes. Remove and drain.

5. Return to the oil and cook for a further 1 minute. Drain well on kitchen paper.

TIME: Preparation takes about 15 minutes and cooking takes 3 minutes per batch.

COOK'S TIP: Fry the prawn balls in batches if necessary.

SERVING IDEAS: Serve with a good quality soy sauce, ketchup or chilli sauce as dips.

Eggs Baked in Tarragon Cream

Extremely quick and easy to make, this is a very tasty way of cooking eggs for either a quick snack or a starter.

SERVES 4

1 knob of butter
4 large eggs
1 tbsp chopped fresh tarragon
Salt and pepper
60ml/4 tbsps cream

1. Butter 4 individual ovenproof ramekins, and break an egg into each one.

2. In a small bowl, stir the chopped tarragon and salt and pepper into the cream and mix well.

3. Spoon 1 tbsp of the cream mixture onto each egg.

4. Put the ramekins onto a baking sheet and cook in a preheated oven, 180°C/350°F/Gas Mark 4 for about 6-8 minutes, until set. Serve immediately.

TIME: Preparation takes about 5 minutes, and cooking takes up to 8 minutes.

PREPARATION: When cooking the eggs, check them during the cooking time to see how hard they have become. If you cook them for 8 minutes, they will be very set. If you require a softer yolk, cook them for a shorter time.

SERVING IDEAS: Serve piping hot with buttered toast or crusty French bread.

FENNEL AND ORANGE CROUSTADE

A delicious mixture which is simple to prepare and suitable to serve at a dinner party.

SERVES 4

4 × 2.5cm/1-inch thick slices wholemeal bread
Oil for deep frying
2 fennel bulbs (reserve any fronds)
4 oranges
1 tbsp olive oil
Pinch salt
Chopped fresh mint for garnishing

1. Trim the crusts off the bread and cut into 7.5cm/3-inch squares.

2. Hollow out the middles, leaving evenly shaped cases.

3. Heat the oil in a deep fat fryer or large saucepan, and deep fry the bread until golden brown.

4. Drain the bread well on absorbent kitchen paper, and leave to cool.

5. Trim the fennel bulbs and slice thinly. Place in a mixing bowl.

6. Remove all the peel and pith from the oranges. Cut flesh into segments – do this over the mixing bowl to catch the juice.

7. Mix the orange segments with the fennel.

8. Add the olive oil and salt and mix together thoroughly.

9. Just before serving, divide the fennel and orange mixture evenly between the bread cases and garnish with fresh mint and fennel fronds.

TIME: Preparation takes 15 minutes, cooking takes 5 minutes.

VARIATIONS: Serve the salad on individual plates sprinkled with croutons.

COOK'S TIP: The salad can be made in advance and refrigerated until required, but do not fill the cases until just before serving.

Melon and Prosciutto

This is one of the best-loved Italian starters. It deserves to be, because the flavour of a ripe melon and the richness of Italian ham complement one another perfectly.

SERVES 4

1 large ripe melon
16 thin slices prosciutto ham

1. Cut the melon in half lengthways, scoop out the seeds and discard them.

2. Cut the melon into quarters and carefully pare off the rind. Cut each quarter into four slices.

3. Wrap each slice of melon in a slice of prosciutto and place on a serving dish. Alternatively, place the melon slices on the dish and cover with the slices of prosciutto, leaving the ends of the melon showing. Serve immediately.

TIME: Preparation takes about 20 minutes.

VARIATIONS: Place the slices of prosciutto flat on serving plates or roll them up into cigar shapes. Serve with quartered fresh figs instead of melon.

COOK'S TIP: Only use melon which is ripe for this recipe, or the flavour will be insipid.

Smoked Salmon Rolls with Prawn Filling

This simply delicious starter will ensure guests feel spoiled without too much effort from the cook.

SERVES 4

225g/8oz frozen or fresh shelled, cooked prawns
2 tbsps mayonnaise
1 tbsp whipped cream
2 tbsps tomato purée
Squeeze lemon juice
8 slices of smoked salmon, about 30g/1oz each
Lemon wedges, sliced cucumber and tomato for garnish

1. Defrost the prawns and drain, if using frozen prawns.

2. Mix the mayonnaise, cream, tomato purée and lemon juice in a bowl and fold in the prawns.

3. Divide the mixture between the 8 slices of smoked salmon, placing it on top in a wedge shape and rolling the salmon around it in a cone shape. Allow two for each person.

4. Garnish with lemon wedges and sliced cucumber and tomato. Serve with thinly sliced soda bread and butter.

TIME: Preparation takes 15 minutes.

SERVING IDEAS: Serve on its own as a starter, or with bread and salad for a light lunch or supper.

SPINACH GNOCCHI

Gnocchi are dumplings that are served like pasta. A dish of gnocchi can be served as a first course or as a light main course, sprinkled with cheese or accompanied by a sauce.

SERVES 4-6

120g/4oz chopped, frozen spinach, defrosted
225g/8oz ricotta cheese
90g/3oz Parmesan cheese
Salt and pepper
Freshly grated nutmeg
1 egg, slightly beaten
45g/1½oz butter

1. Press the spinach between two plates to extract all the moisture.

2. Mix the spinach with the ricotta cheese, half the Parmesan cheese, salt, pepper and nutmeg. Gradually add the egg, beating well until the mixture holds together when shaped.

3. With floured hands, shape the mixture into ovals using about 1 tbsp mixture for each gnocchi.

4. Lower into simmering water, 3 or 4 at a time, and allow to cook gently until the gnocchi float to the surface, about 1-2 minutes.

5. Remove with a draining spoon and place in a well buttered ovenproof dish.

6. When all the gnocchi are cooked, sprinkle on the remaining Parmesan cheese and dot with the remaining butter.

7. Reheat for 10 minutes in an oven, preheated to 200°C/400°F/Gas Mark 6, and brown under a pre-heated grill before serving.

TIME: Preparation takes about 15 minutes, cooking takes about 20 minutes.

SERVING IDEAS: Accompany with a tomato or cheese sauce for a light meal with a salad and hot bread.

COOK'S TIP: Gnocchi are best served soon after they are cooked. If allowed to stand overnight they become very heavy.

Stuffed Eggs

Stuffed eggs makes an attractive, and deliciously different, party appetiser.

MAKES 36

18 small eggs, or quail eggs
60g/2oz unsalted butter
1 clove garlic, crushed
90g/3oz cooked, peeled prawns, finely chopped
½ tsp finely chopped fresh basil
Freshly ground black pepper, to taste

1. Cook the eggs in boiling water for 5 minutes. Drain, and plunge them immediately into cold water.

2. Allow the eggs to cool completely, then remove the shells. Rinse and drain.

3. Cut each egg in half lengthways and carefully remove the yolks.

4. Put the yolks into a large bowl and beat in the butter and garlic. Mix well. This, and the next step, could be carried out in a food processor.

5. Add the prawns, basil and pepper to the creamed egg yolk mixture. Beat thoroughly until a soft consistency results.

6. Fill each egg white half with a little of the prepared mixture, piling it attractively into the cavity left by the egg yolk.

7. Refrigerate until required.

TIME: Preparation takes 15 minutes, cooking takes 5 minutes.

VARIATIONS: Use flaked white crab meat instead of the prawns. For a more exotic dish, use quail eggs instead of hens' eggs.

SERVING IDEAS: Serve the filled egg halves on a plate which has been garnished with frisée lettuce leaves, and tiny pieces of red pepper.

Quick Liver Pâté

Liver sausage is lightly seasoned and smoked, and is available with either a smooth or coarse consistancy.
It makes an "instant" pâté.

SERVES 4

300g/11oz German liver sausage
60g/2oz melted butter, preferably unsalted
2 tbsps brandy (optional)
1 clove garlic, crushed
Salt and pepper
Salad, cress and black olives for garnish

1. Place the sausage in a bowl with the butter, brandy, if using, garlic, salt and pepper and beat until smooth. Alternatively, use a food processor.

2. Pour the mixture into a piping bag fitted with a rosette nozzle.

3. Choose a large serving dish or individual plates and pipe out several swirls of pâté. Garnish with sliced or whole black olives, salad and cress.

TIME: Preparation takes about 15 minutes.

COOK'S TIP: Always squeeze out the mixture from the top of the piping bag down to the nozzle. If the bag is held in the middle, the mixture will soften and melt or it will burst out of the top.

SERVING IDEAS: Serve with hot toast fingers or thin slices of buttered rye bread. Instead of piping the pâté, serve in individual pots.

Mushrooms in Sour Cream

This very old recipe originally called for freshly gathered forest mushrooms.

SERVES 4-6

450g/1lb button mushrooms, quartered
30g/1oz butter or margarine
6 spring onions, thinly sliced
1 tbsp flour
1 tbsp lemon juice
2 tbsps chopped fresh dill or 1 tbsp dried dill
Pinch salt and pepper
90ml/3 fl oz sour cream
Paprika

1. Rinse the mushrooms and pat dry well. Trim the stalks level with the caps before quartering. Melt the butter in a frying pan and add the mushrooms and onions. Sauté for about 1 minute and stir in the flour.

2. Add the lemon juice and all the remaining ingredients, except the sour cream and paprika, and cook slowly for about 1 minute.

3. Stir in the sour cream and adjust the seasoning. Heat through for about 1 minute. Spoon into individual serving dishes or on top of buttered toast. Sprinkle with paprika and serve immediately.

TIME: Preparation takes about 20 minutes, cooking takes about 5-7 minutes.

WATCHPOINT: Sour cream will curdle if boiled, although the addition of flour to the sauce will help to stabilise it somewhat.

SERVING IDEAS: Use as a side dish or a starter with meat, poultry or game. Prepare double quantity and serve with a salad and bread as a light lunch.

Mussels in Ginger-Cumin Sauce

This delicious combination of seafood, wine and spices makes for a mouthwatering start to a meal.

SERVES 4

1kg/2¼lbs mussels in their shells, scraped
2 shallots, chopped
1 bay leaf
90ml/3 fl oz white wine
30g/1oz butter
1 small piece ginger, grated
½ tsp cumin
¼ tsp turmeric
½ green chilli, seeded and chopped
Juice of ½ lime
140ml/¼ pint cream
Salt and pepper
2 tbsps chopped parsley

1. Discard any mussels that are open or have cracked shells.

2. Put mussels into a large, deep pan and sprinkle over half the shallot. Add the bay leaf and wine.

3. Cover the pan and bring to the boil, shaking the pan. Cook for about 3 minutes or until the mussels have opened. Set aside and keep covered.

4. Melt the butter in a saucepan and add the remaining chopped shallot. Soften for 2 minutes and add the ginger, cumin, turmeric and chilli.

5. Add the lime juice and strain on the cooking liquid from the mussels. Bring to the boil, stirring occasionally and allow to boil to reduce by half.

6. Pour on the cream and reboil to reduce slightly and thicken.

7. Divide the mussels between 4 serving bowls and pour on the sauce.

8. Sprinkle parsley over each serving.

TIME: Preparation takes 20 minutes and cooking takes about 15 minutes.

SERVING IDEAS: Serve with wholemeal French bread.

COOK'S TIP: Double the ingredients to serve 4 as a main course.

Pasta Shells with Seafood

This speedy meal is excellent for informal entertaining.

SERVES 4

60g/2oz butter or margarine
2 cloves garlic, crushed
75ml/5 tbsps dry white wine
280ml/½ pint single cream
1 tbsp cornflour
2 tbsps water
1 tbsp lemon juice
Salt and pepper
275g/10oz pasta shells
450g/1lb prawns, shelled and de-veined
120g/4oz scallops, cleaned and sliced
1 tbsp chopped parsley

1. Melt the butter in a pan. Add the garlic, and cook for 1 minute. Add the wine and cream, bring back to the boil, and cook for 2 minutes.

2. Mix the cornflour with the water, and pour into the sauce. Stir until boiling. Add the lemon juice and salt and pepper to taste.

3. Meanwhile, cook the pasta in plenty of boiling, salted water, for about 10 minutes, until tender. Drain, shaking to remove excess water.

4. Add the prawns and scallops to the sauce and cook for 3 minutes.

5. Pour the sauce over the pasta shells, toss, and garnish with parsley before serving.

TIME: Preparation takes 5 minutes, cooking takes 15 minutes.

BUYING GUIDE: When buying fresh prawns ensure they are firm and brightly coloured.

Turkey Marsala

Marsala is a dessert wine from Sicily which also complements turkey, veal or chicken surprisingly well. It is traditional, but sherry will serve as a substitute if Marsala is unavailable.

SERVES 4

4 turkey escalopes or breast fillets
60g/2oz butter or margarine
1 clove garlic
4 anchovy fillets, soaked in milk
4 slices Mozzarella cheese
Capers
2 tsps chopped marjoram
1 tbsp chopped parsley
3 tbsps Marsala
140ml/¼ pint double cream
Salt and pepper

1. If using the turkey breasts, flatten between two sheets of greaseproof paper with a meat mallet or rolling pin.

2. Melt butter in a frying pan and, when foaming, add the garlic and the turkey. Cook for a few minutes on each side until lightly browned. Remove them from the pan.

3. Drain the anchovy fillets and rinse them well. Dry on kitchen paper. Put a slice of cheese on top of each turkey fillet and arrange the anchovies and capers on top of each. Sprinkle with the chopped herbs and return the turkey to the pan.

4. Cook the turkey a further 5 minutes over moderate heat, until the turkey is cooked through, and the cheese has melted. Remove to a serving dish and keep warm.

5. Return the pan to the heat and add the Marsala to deglaze, then reduce the heat. Add the cream and whisk in well. Lower the heat and simmer gently, uncovered, for a few minutes to thicken the sauce. Season the sauce with salt and pepper and spoon over the turkey fillets to serve.

TIME: Preparation takes about 25 minutes and cooking about 15 minutes.

WATCHPOINT: Turkey breast fillets are very lean so can dry out easily if over-cooked.

SERVING IDEAS: Accompany the Turkey Marsala with new potatoes and lightly cooked courgettes.

Trout with Chive Sauce

Chive sauce really complements trout and turns a simple dish into a speedy meal fit for a special occasion.

SERVES 4

4 even-sized rainbow trout, gutted and fins trimmed
Flour mixed with salt and pepper for dredging
45g/1½oz butter, melted
2 tbsps white wine
280ml/½ pint double cream
1 small bunch chives, snipped
Salt and pepper

1. Dredge the trout with the seasoned flour and place on a lightly greased baking sheet. Spoon the melted butter over the fish.

2. Bake in a 200°C/400°F/Gas Mark 6 oven for about 10 minutes, basting frequently with the butter. Cook until the skin is crisp. Check the fish on the underside close to the bone. If the fish is not cooked through, lower the oven temperature to 160°C/325°F/ Gas Mark 3 for a further 5 minutes.

3. Pour the wine into a small saucepan and bring to the boil. Boil to reduce by half. Pour on the cream and bring back to the boil. Allow to boil rapidly until the cream thickens slightly. Stir in the snipped chives, reserving some to sprinkle on top, if wished.

4. When the fish are browned remove to a serving dish and spoon over some of the sauce. Sprinkle with the reserved chives and serve the rest of the sauce separately.

TIME: Preparation takes 15 minutes and cooking takes 15-20 minutes.

VARIATIONS: Use this sauce with other fish such as salmon steaks.

SERVING IDEAS: Serve with boiled new potatoes and broccoli.

Beef Stroganoff

This classic recipe is quick and easy to prepare, but it does require the best quality beef.

SERVES 4

675g/1½lbs rump or fillet steak
120g/4oz butter
1 medium onion, thinly sliced
225g/8oz mushrooms, sliced
30g/1oz flour
1 tbsp tomato purée
280ml/10 fl oz good beef stock
Salt
Freshly ground black pepper
140ml/¼ pint soured cream
1 tbsp finely chopped parsley

1. Cut the meat into strips approximately 7.5 × 2.5cm/3-× 1-inch.

2. Melt 30g/1oz of the butter in a large pan and fry the onion for 3-4 minutes until soft. Remove the onion and add the meat a little at a time until it is sealed on all sides, remove the meat to a plate.

3. Add the rest of the butter and fry the mushrooms for 2-3 minutes, then remove from the pan.

4. Stir the flour into the pan juices, followed by the tomato purée and cook for 1 minute. Add the stock, and stir continuously until smooth.

5. Return the steak, mushrooms and onion to the pan, add the seasoning and heat through thoroughly.

6. Transfer to a warm serving dish and gently stir in the soured cream, creating a marbled effect. Sprinkle with chopped parsley.

TIME: Preparation takes about 10 minutes and cooking takes 15-20 minutes.

SERVING IDEAS: Accompany with boiled rice or creamed potatoes, and broccoli.

COD CURRY

The fragrant spices used in this recipe are now readily available at most supermarkets.

SERVES 4

1 large onion, chopped
3 tbsps vegetable oil
2.5cm/1-inch piece cinnamon stick
1 bay leaf
1 tsp ginger paste
1 tsp garlic paste
1 tsp chilli powder
1 tsp ground cumin
1 tsp ground coriander
¼ tsp ground turmeric
140ml/¼ pint natural yogurt
 or 225g/8oz can tomatoes, chopped
1-2 fresh green chillies, chopped
2 sprigs fresh coriander leaves, chopped
1lb cod cutlets, or fillets, cut into 5cm/2-inch pieces
1 tsp salt

1. In a large heavy-based saucepan, sauté the onion in the oil until golden brown. Add the cinnamon, bay leaf and the ginger and garlic pastes and cook for 1 minute.

2. Add the ground spices and cook for a further minute, then stir in *either* the yogurt, *or* the canned tomatoes and the chopped chillies and coriander leaves.

3. Only if you have used yogurt, stir in 140ml/¼ pint water and simmer the mixture for 2-3 minutes. Do not add any water if you have used the canned tomatoes.

4. Stir the cod into the sauce, and add the salt. Cover the pan and simmer for 15-18 minutes before serving.

TIME: Preparation takes about 15 minutes, and cooking takes about 20 minutes.

COOK'S TIP: Great care should be taken when preparing fresh chillies. Always wash hands thoroughly afterwards, and avoid getting any juice in the eyes or mouth. Rinse with copious amounts of clear water if this happens. For a milder curry, remove the seeds.

SERVING IDEAS: Serve with boiled rice and a cucumber salad.

Barbecued Prawns

It's the sauce rather than the cooking method that gives the dish its name. It's spicy, zippy and hot.

SERVES 2

450g/1lb large prawns, cooked and unpeeled
120g/4oz unsalted butter
1 tsp each white, black and cayenne pepper
Pinch salt
1 tsp each chopped fresh thyme, rosemary and marjoram
1 clove garlic, crushed
1 tsp Worcestershire sauce
140ml/¼ pint fish stock
60ml/4 tbsps dry white wine
Cooked rice, to serve

1. Remove the eyes and the legs from the prawns.

2. Melt the butter in a large frying pan and add the white pepper, black pepper, cayenne pepper, salt, herbs and garlic. Add the prawns and toss over heat for a few minutes until heated through. Remove the prawns and set them aside and keep warm.

3. Add the Worcestershire sauce, stock and wine to the ingredients in the pan. Bring to the boil and cook for about 3 minutes to reduce. Add salt to taste.

4. Arrange the prawns on a bed of rice and pour over the sauce to serve.

TIME: Preparation takes about 15 minutes and cooking takes about 5 minutes.

PREPARATION: Because the prawns are precooked, cook them very briefly again, just to heat through. Use uncooked, unpeeled prawns if possible. Cook these until they curl and turn pink.

SERVING IDEAS: The prawns may also be served cold. If serving cold, prepare the sauce with 90ml/6 tbsps oil instead of the butter.

Liver Veneziana

As the name indicates, this recipe originated in Venice. The lemon juice offsets the rich taste of liver in this very famous Italian dish.

SERVES 4-6

Risotto
45g/1½oz butter or margarine
1 large onion, chopped
250g/9oz Italian (risotto) rice
60ml/4 tbsps dry white wine
570ml/1 pint chicken stock
¼ tsp saffron
Salt and pepper
2 tbsps grated fresh Parmesan cheese

Liver
450g/1lb calves' or lambs' liver
Flour for dredging
30g/1oz butter or margarine
2 tbsps oil
3 onions, thinly sliced
Juice of ½ a lemon
Salt and pepper
1 tbsp chopped parsley

1. Melt the butter for the risotto in a large frying pan, add the onion and cook until soft but not coloured, over gentle heat.

2. Add the rice and cook for about a minute until the rice looks transparent.

3. Add the wine, stock, saffron and seasoning. Stir well and bring to the boil. Lower the heat and cook gently for about 20 minutes, stirring frequently, until the liquid has been absorbed.

4. Meanwhile, heat the butter or margarine and 1 tbsp oil in a large frying pan, and cook the onions until golden.

5. Trim the liver and cut into strips. Toss in a sieve with the flour to coat.

6. Remove the onions from the pan to a plate. Add more oil if necessary, raise the heat under the pan and add the liver. Cook, stirring constantly, for about 2 minutes.

7. Return the onions and add the lemon juice and parsley. Cook a further 2 minutes or until the liver is tender. Season with salt and pepper and serve with the risotto.

8. To finish the risotto, add the cheese and salt and pepper to taste when the liquid has been absorbed, and toss to melt the cheese.

TIME: Risotto takes about 30 minutes to prepare and cook. Liver takes about 4 minutes to cook.

WATCHPOINT: Liver needs only brief cooking or it will toughen.

PREPARATION: Tossing the liver and flour together in a sieve coats each piece of meat more evenly than can be done by hand.

COOK'S TIP: If wished add 60ml/4 tbsps stock to the recipe for a little more sauce.

SKATE IN BUTTER SAUCE

This is a lovely tasting fish that is often neglected. Once you try it, though you'll serve it often.

SERVES 4

4 wings of skate
1 slice onion
2 parsley stalks
Pinch salt
6 black peppercorns

Beurre Noir
60g/2oz butter
2 tbsps white wine vinegar
1 tbsp capers
1 tbsp chopped parsley (optional)

1. Place the skate in one layer in a large, deep pan. Completely cover with water and add the onion, parsley stalks, salt and peppercorns. Bring gently to the boil with the pan uncovered. Allow to simmer 15-20 minutes, or until the skate is done.

2. Lift the fish out onto a serving dish and remove the skin and any large pieces of bone. Take care not to break up the fish.

3. Place the butter in a small pan and cook over high heat until it begins to brown. Add the capers and immediately remove the butter from the heat. Add the vinegar, which will cause the butter to bubble. Add parsley, if using, and pour immediately over the fish to serve.

TIME: Preparation takes about 5 minutes, cooking takes 15-20 minutes for the fish and about 5 minutes to brown the butter.

VARIATIONS: Chopped black olives, shallots or mushrooms may be used instead of, or in addition to, the capers. Add lemon juice instead of vinegar, if wished.

COOK'S TIP: When the skate is done, it will pull away from the bones in long strips.

Smoked Salmon Roma

This quick dish has a fresh, light tasting sauce, perfect for summer eating. A simple green salad goes well.

SERVES 4

1 small onion, chopped
A little butter and oil for frying
2 courgettes, cut into sticks
Small bunch fresh dill, chopped
225ml/8 fl oz single cream mixed with
2 tbsps of soured cream
Salt and black pepper
120g/4oz smoked salmon, cut into strips
225g/8oz fine ribbon pasta (linguine)
Lemon and dill to decorate

1. Fry the onion in a little butter and oil until soft.

2. Add the courgettes and sauté for a few minutes. Do not overcook, they should remain crisp.

3. Add the chopped dill and the cream mixture, and gently heat through.

4. Season to taste and fold in the salmon strips. Keep warm.

5. Cook the pasta as directed on packet; drain.

6. Put the pasta in an oval dish and pour the sauce into the centre. Decorate with lemon wedges and dill.

TIME: Preparation and cooking takes about 25 minutes.

VARIATIONS: Use different shapes of pasta such as bows, or whatever you have to hand.

Oven Baked Spaghetti

A convenient way to cook this favourite mid-week meal.

SERVES 4

225g/8oz wholewheat spaghetti, cooked
2 x 400g/14oz tins tomatoes, roughly chopped
1 large onion, grated
1 tsp oregano
Seasoning
120g/4oz Cheddar cheese
2 tbsps grated Parmesan cheese

1. Grease four individual ovenproof dishes and place a quarter of the spaghetti in each one.

2. Pour the tomatoes over the top.

3. Add the onion, sprinkle with oregano and season well.

4. Slice the cheese finely and arrange over the top of the spaghetti mixture.

5. Sprinkle with Parmesan and bake at 180°C/350°F/Gas Mark 4 for 20-25 minutes.

TIME: Preparation takes 10 minutes, cooking takes 20-25 minutes.

SERVING IDEAS: Serve with garlic bread.

WATCHPOINT: When cooking spaghetti remember to add a few drops of oil to the boiling water to stop it sticking together.

COOK'S TIP: Oven Baked Spaghetti may be cooked in one large casserole if required, but add 10 minutes to the cooking time.

PRAWNS AND GINGER

Quick and easy to prepare, this dish is really delicious and also very nutritious.

SERVES 6

2 tbsps oil
675g/1½lbs peeled prawns
2.5cm/1-inch piece fresh root ginger, peeled and finely chopped
2 cloves of garlic, peeled and finely chopped
2-3 spring onions, chopped
1 leek, white part only, cut into strips
120g/4oz peas, shelled
175g/6oz bean sprouts
2 tbsps dark soy sauce
1 tsp sugar
Pinch salt

1. Heat the oil in a wok and stir-fry the prawns for 2-3 minutes. Set the prawns aside.

2. Reheat the oil and add the ginger and garlic. Stir quickly, then add the onions, leek and peas. Stir-fry for 2-3 minutes.

3. Add the bean sprouts and prawns to the cooked vegetables. Stir in the soy sauce, sugar and salt, and cook for 2 minutes. Serve immediately.

TIME: Preparation takes about 10 minutes, and cooking takes about 7-9 minutes.

PREPARATION: The vegetables can be prepared in advance and kept in airtight plastic boxes in the refrigerator for up to 6 hours before needed.

SERVING IDEAS: Serve this on its own with rice or pasta, or as part of an authentic Chinese meal.

Spaghetti Marinara

A delightful mix of seafood makes this dish special enough for any occasion, and it's quick and easy too!

SERVES 4

45g/1½oz can anchovy fillets
75ml/5 tbsps water
75ml/5 tbsps dry white wine
1 bay leaf
4 peppercorns
225g/8oz scallops, cleaned and sliced
2 tbsps olive oil
2 cloves garlic, crushed
1 tsp basil
1 x 400g/14oz can plum tomatoes, seeded and chopped
1 tbsp tomato purée
275g/10oz spaghetti
450g/1lb cooked prawns, shelled and de-veined
1 tbsp chopped parsley
Salt and pepper

1. Drain anchovies and cut into small pieces.

2. Place water, wine, bay leaf and peppercorns in a pan. Heat to a slow boil. Add scallops and cook for 2 minutes. Remove and drain.

3. Heat the oil, add garlic and basil, and cook for 30 seconds. Add tomatoes, anchovies and tomato purée. Stir until combined. Cook for 10 minutes.

4. Meanwhile, cook the spaghetti in a large pan of boiling, salted water for 10 minutes, or until tender but still firm. Drain.

5. Add seafood to sauce, and cook a further 1 minute, to heat through. Add parsley and stir through. Season with salt and pepper to taste. Toss gently.

6. Pour sauce over spaghetti and serve immediately, sprinkled with parsley.

TIME: Preparation takes 10 minutes, cooking takes 20 minutes.

VARIATIONS: Substitute the prawns and scallops with the fresh seafood 'cocktails' now available in many supermarkets.

CORONATION CHICKEN

Supposedly invented for the Coronation of Queen Elizabeth II, this dish is excellent for summer parties or lunches, particularly as so much of it can be prepared in advance.

SERVES 6

5-6 cooked chicken breasts, cut into chunks

Curry Mayonnaise
2 tbsps olive oil
1 small onion, finely chopped
1 level tbsp curry powder
140ml/¼ pint chicken stock
1 large tsp tomato purée
Juice of ½ lemon
2 level tbsps apricot jam or sweet chutney
280ml/½ pint mayonnaise
3 tbsps double cream

1. Heat the oil in a saucepan, add the chopped onion, cover and fry gently for 5 minutes until the onion is soft.

2. Stir in the curry powder and cook, stirring, for a further 2 minutes to bring out the flavour.

3. Stir in the stock, tomato purée, lemon juice and jam or chutney. Stir until boiling, then cook for 5 minutes until the mixture reduces and thickens.

4. Allow to cool and then stir in the mayonnaise and cream. The sauce should be of a coating consistency.

5. Arrange chicken pieces in a serving dish and spoon the sauce over.

TIME: Preparation takes 15-20 minutes.

SERVING IDEAS: A rice salad with pineapple, green pepper and sultanas goes well with this dish.

Ham and Green Pepper Omelette

Served with salad and crusty French bread, this makes a tasty lunch or supper dish.

MAKES 1

3 eggs
2 tbsps milk
Freshly ground black pepper
1 tbsp vegetable oil
30g/1oz chopped green pepper
2 tomatoes, skinned, seeded and roughly chopped
60g/2oz lean ham, cut into small dice

1. Break the eggs into a bowl and beat in the milk and pepper.

2. Heat the oil in an omelette pan and cook the green pepper until it is just soft.

3. Stir in the tomatoes and the ham. Heat through for 1 minute.

4. Pour the egg mixture into the frying pan over the vegetables. Stir the mixture briskly with a wooden spoon, until it begins to cook.

5. As the egg begins to set, lift it slightly and tilt the pan to allow the uncooked egg to flow underneath.

6. When the egg on top is still slightly creamy, fold the omelette in half and slip it onto a serving plate. Serve immediately.

TIME: Preparation takes about 15 minutes, cooking takes 5 minutes.

COOK'S TIP: To skin tomatoes easily, cut a small cross into the skin and drop them into boiling water for about 10 seconds, then plunge into cold water. This loosens the skin.

VARIATIONS: Use any selection of your favourite vegetables to vary this delicious dish.

Rich Pan-Fried Steaks

Thin steaks are quickly fried and then cooked in a savoury brown sauce.

SERVES 4

4-8 pieces frying steak, depending on size
1 tbsp oil
1 tbsp butter or margarine
1 tbsp flour
6 spring onions
1 clove garlic, crushed
1 tsp chopped thyme
2 tsps chopped parsley
3 tomatoes, skinned, seeded and chopped
280ml/½ pint beef stock
Dash of Tabasco
Salt and pepper

1. Place the meat between 2 sheets of greaseproof or waxed paper and pound with a rolling pin or a meat mallet to flatten slightly.

2. Heat the oil in a large frying pan and brown the meat quickly, a few pieces at a time. Set the meat aside.

3. Melt the butter or margarine in the frying pan and add the flour. Cut the white part off the spring onions and chop it finely. Add to the flour and butter, reserving the green tops for later use.

4. Add the garlic to the pan and cook the mixture slowly, stirring frequently until it is a dark golden brown. Add the herbs, tomatoes, stock, Tabasco and salt and pepper to taste, and bring to the boil. Cook for about 5 minutes to thicken and then add the steaks. Cook to heat the meat through.

5. Chop the green tops of the spring onions and sprinkle over the steaks to garnish.

TIME: Preparation takes about 20 minutes and cooking takes about 20 minutes.

SERVING IDEAS: Serve with rice or potatoes. Add a green vegetable or salad.

VARIATIONS: Add chopped red or green pepper to the sauce.

Sautéed Lemon Pork

A perfect way to prepare this tender cut of pork. Butchers will bat out the meat for you.

SERVES 4

8 small pork escalopes or steaks, batted out until thin
Flour for dredging
Salt and pepper
30g/1oz butter or margarine
1 green pepper, thinly sliced
90ml/6 tbsps dry white wine or sherry
1 tbsp lemon juice
175ml/6 fl oz chicken stock
1 lemon, peeled and thinly sliced

1. Dredge pork with a mixture of flour, salt and pepper. Shake off the excess.

2. Melt the butter or margarine in a large frying pan and brown the pork, a few pieces at a time. Remove the meat and keep it warm.

3. Cook the peppers briefly and set aside with the pork.

4. Pour the wine or sherry and lemon juice into the pan to deglaze. Add the stock and bring to the boil. Boil for 5 minutes to reduce. Add the pork and peppers and cook for 15 minutes over gentle heat. Add the lemon slices and heat through before serving.

TIME: Preparation takes about 25 minutes and cooking takes about 20-25 minutes.

PREPARATION: Cut off all the rind and pith of the lemon, using a sharp knife, before slicing the flesh.

VARIATIONS: Use red pepper instead of green pepper and add chopped spring onions.

Macaroni Cheese with Anchovies

Anchovies add extra flavour to this much loved homely dish.

SERVES 4

60g/2oz can anchovy fillets
225g/8oz macaroni
60g/2oz butter or margarine
60g/2oz flour
570ml/1 pint milk
½ tsp dry mustard
175g/6oz Gruyère or Cheddar cheese, grated
Salt and pepper

1. Drain the anchovies, and set enough aside to slice to make a thin lattice over the dish. Chop the rest finely.

2. Cook the macaroni in plenty of boiling, salted water for 10 minutes, or until tender but still firm. Rinse in hot water and drain well.

3. Meanwhile, melt the butter in a pan. Stir in the flour and cook for 1 minute.

4. Remove from the heat, and gradually stir in the milk. Return to the heat and bring to the boil. Simmer for 3 minutes, stirring occasionally.

5. Stir in the mustard, anchovies, and half the cheese. Season with salt and pepper to taste. Stir in the macaroni, and pour into an ovenproof dish.

6. Sprinkle the remaining cheese over the top, and make a latticework with the remaining anchovies. Brown under a hot grill. Serve immediately.

TIME: Preparation takes 5 minutes, cooking takes 15 minutes.

SERVING IDEAS: Serve this hearty dish with crusty bread and a mixed green salad.

Chicken with Cherries

Canned cherries make an easy sauce that really dresses up chicken.

SERVES 6

Oil
6 chicken breasts, skinned and boned
1 sprig fresh rosemary
Grated rind and juice of ½ a lemon
140ml/¼ pint red wine
Salt and pepper
450g/1lb canned black cherries, pitted
2 tsps cornflour

1. Heat about 60ml/4 tbsps oil in a frying pan over moderate heat. Place in the chicken breasts, skinned side down first. Cook until just lightly browned. Turn over and cook the second side about 2 minutes.

2. Remove any oil remaining in the pan and add the rosemary, lemon rind, wine and salt and pepper. Bring to the boil and then lower the heat.

3. Add the cherries and their juice. Cook, covered, for 15 minutes or until the chicken is tender. Remove the chicken and cherries and keep them warm. Discard the rosemary.

4. Mix the cornflour and lemon juice. Add several spoonfuls of the hot sauce to the cornflour mixture. Return the mixture to the frying pan and bring to the boil, stirring constantly, until thickened and cleared.

5. Pour the sauce over the chicken and cherries. Heat through and serve.

TIME: Preparation takes about 10 minutes and cooking takes about 20 minutes.

PREPARATION: Serve the chicken dish on the day that it is cooked – it does not keep well.

SERVING IDEAS: Serve with plain boiled rice. Accompany with a green vegetable such as lightly steamed mange tout.

Veal Scaloppine with Prosciutto and Cheese

Veal is the meat used most often in Italian cooking. Good veal is tender and quick cooking, but expensive. Save this recipe for your next dinner party!

SERVES 4

8 veal escalopes
30g/1oz butter or margarine
1 clove garlic, crushed
8 slices prosciutto ham
3 tbsps sherry
140ml/¼ pint beef stock
1 sprig rosemary
8 slices Mozzarella cheese
Salt and pepper

1. Pound the veal escalopes out thinly between two pieces of greaseproof paper with a meat mallet or a rolling pin.

2. Melt the butter or margarine in a frying pan and add the veal and garlic. Cook until the veal is lightly browned on both sides.

3. Place a piece of prosciutto on top of each piece of veal and add the sherry, stock and sprig of rosemary to the pan. Cover the pan and cook the veal for about 10 minutes over gentle heat or until tender and cooked through.

4. Remove the meat to a warmed heatproof serving dish and top each piece of veal with a slice of cheese.

5. Bring the cooking liquid from the veal to the boil, season and allow to boil rapidly to reduce slightly.

6. Meanwhile, grill the veal to melt and brown the cheese. Remove the sprig of rosemary from the sauce and pour the sauce around the meat to serve.

TIME: Preparation takes about 15 minutes, cooking takes 15-20 minutes.

VARIATIONS: White wine may be substituted for the sherry, if wished, and 1 tsp of tomato purée may be added to the sauce. Use chicken, turkey or pork instead of the veal.

Crunchy Cod

Cod provides the perfect base for a crunchy, slightly spicy topping.

SERVES 4

4 even-sized cod fillets
Salt and pepper
90g/3oz butter, melted
90g/3oz dry breadcrumbs
1 tsp dry mustard
1 tsp finely chopped onion
Dash Worcestershire sauce and Tabasco
2 tbsps lemon juice
1 tbsp finely chopped parsley

1. Season the fish fillets with salt and pepper and place them on a grill pan. Brush with some of the butter and grill for about 5 minutes.

2. Combine the remaining butter with the breadcrumbs, mustard, onion, Worcestershire sauce, Tabasco, lemon juice and parsley.

3. Spoon the mixture carefully on top of each fish fillet, covering it completely. Press down lightly to pack the crumbs into place. Grill for a further 5-7 minutes, or until the top is lightly browned and the fish flakes.

TIME: Preparation takes about 15 minutes and cooking takes about 12 minutes.

PREPARATION: If wished, the fish may also be baked in the oven at 180°C/350°F/Gas Mark 4. Cover the fish with foil for the first 5 minutes of baking time, uncover and top with the breadcrumb mixture. Bake for a further 10-12 minutes.

VARIATIONS: The breadcrumb topping may be used on other fish such as haddock, halibut or sole.

Liver with Onions

This dish is simple to prepare, but absolutely delicious and highly nutritious.

SERVES 4-6

450g/1lb onions
450g/1lb lambs' liver, thinly sliced
Salt and freshly ground black pepper
45g/1½oz plain flour
3 tbsps vegetable oil
30g/1oz butter
2 tbsps fresh chopped parsley

1. Peel the onions and slice thinly, keeping each slice in circles if possible.

2. Trim away any large tubes from the liver using a pair of small scissors or a sharp knife.

3. Mix the seasoning and the flour together on a plate and turn the liver in the mixture to coat the slices evenly.

4. Gently heat the oil and the butter in a large frying pan until foaming.

5. Add the onion and sauté until just golden.

6. Add the liver slices and sauté for 3-5 minutes on each side until well cooked. Cooking time will depend on the thickness of each slice.

7. Stir the parsley into the liver and onions and serve immediately on hot plates.

TIME: Preparation takes 15 minutes, cooking takes about 10 minutes.

SERVING IDEAS: Serve with creamed potatoes and green vegetables.

WATCHPOINT: Do not overcook liver, as it will toughen.

Chicken and Avocado Pear Salad with Grapes and Tarragon

A quick and easy summer lunch dish.

SERVES 4-6

4-6 cooked chicken breasts
1-2 ripe avocado pears
2 tbsps lemon juice
140ml/¼ pint mayonnaise
90ml/3 fl oz double cream
1 tbsp chopped fresh tarragon or ½ tsp dried
Salt and freshly ground black pepper
1 crisp lettuce
120g/4oz seedless green grapes

1. Cut the chicken into bite-sized pieces and set aside.

2. Peel and slice the avocados, and sprinkle with the lemon juice. Set aside.

3. Mix the mayonnaise, double cream and tarragon and season to taste with the salt and pepper.

4. Wash and shred the lettuce and put into the bottom of an attractive serving dish.

5. Gently combine the chicken and avocado with the mayonnaise dressing. Pile onto the lettuce and garnish with the green grapes. Serve at once.

TIME: Preparation takes 15-20 minutes.

VARIATIONS: Serve the chicken on a bed of mixed lettuce and herbs.

Broccoli and Cauliflower Salad

Serve this simple salad with crackers.

SERVES 4

1 red pepper
300g/10oz broccoli
300g/10oz cauliflower
1 tbsp roasted almond flakes

Dressing
60ml/4 tbsps Greek yogurt
2 tbsps lemon juice
2 tbsps olive oil
Salt and pepper
Pinch of nutmeg

1. Cut the pepper into matchstick pieces.

2. Wash and trim the broccoli and cauliflower and break into small florets.

3. Place the pepper, broccoli and cauliflower in a mixing bowl.

4. Combine the yogurt, lemon juice, olive oil, seasoning and nutmeg in a screw top jar and shake well.

5. Spoon the dressing over the salad and mix together well.

6. Divide the mixture between 4 individual serving plates and garnish with the almond flakes.

TIME: Preparation takes 10 minutes.

VARIATIONS: Omit the nutmeg from the dressing and add a few freshly chopped herbs.

COOK'S TIP: If preparing this salad in advance, don't garnish with the almonds until serving time.

P
S

KENSINGTON SALAD

This salad has plenty of crunch to it and a lovely tangy dressing.

SERVES 2-3

3 large mushrooms, thinly sliced
1 medium eating apple, cut into chunks and coated with lemon juice
2 celery sticks, cut into matchsticks
30g/1oz walnut pieces
1 bunch watercress

Dressing
1 tbsp mayonnaise
1 tbsp thick yogurt
½ tsp herb mustard
A little lemon juice
Salt and pepper

1. Place the mushrooms, apple, celery and walnuts in a bowl.

2. Combine all the ingredients for the dressing and mix gently with the vegetables.

3. Arrange the watercress on a flat dish or platter and mound the salad mixture on the top.

TIME: Preparation takes about 10 minutes.

VARIATIONS: A medium bulb of fennel, finely sliced, could be used in place of the celery.

SERVING IDEAS: Decorate the top of this salad with a line of sliced strawberries or kiwi fruit.

Greek Country Salad

Lettuce is cut finely for salads in Greece. In fact, the finer the shreds of lettuce the better the salad is considered to be.

SERVES 4

2 tbsps olive oil
1 tbsp lemon juice
Salt and ground black pepper
1 clove garlic, crushed
1 cos lettuce, well washed
3 tomatoes, sliced
90g/3oz black olives
120g/4oz feta cheese, diced
½ red pepper, sliced
6 peperonata
Fresh or dried oregano

1. Whisk the oil, lemon juice, salt and pepper and garlic together until well emulsified. A blender or food processor may be used for this.

2. Stack up 5 or 6 lettuce leaves and shred them finely with a sharp knife.

3. Place the lettuce in the bottom of a serving dish and arrange the other ingredients on top. Spoon over the dressing and sprinkle on the oregano.

TIME: Preparation takes about 10-15 minutes.

BUYING GUIDE: Peperonata are small whole peppers preserved in brine. They can be bought bottled in delicatessens and some supermarkets.

VARIATIONS: Substitute green pepper for red pepper if wished. Other varieties of lettuce may also be used.

Green and Gold Sunflower Salad

This colourful salad makes a spectacular and delicious addition to a summer meal.

SERVES 4

3 tbsps sunflower oil
1 tbsp lemon juice
Salt and pepper
2 large ripe avocados
8 ripe apricots
140ml/¼ pint natural yogurt
2 tsps honey
Grated rind of 1 lemon
2 tsps chopped fresh parsley
1 small webb lettuce, washed and separated into leaves
60g/2oz toasted sunflower seeds

1. Put the oil and lemon juice into a small bowl with the salt and pepper. Mix together well.

2. Cut the avocados in half and remove the stones. Peel them, cut into slices and mix these into the oil and lemon juice dressing very carefully, taking care not to break them.

3. Cut the apricots in half and remove the stones. If the apricots are large, cut them in half again. Add them to the avocados in the dressing.

4. In another bowl, mix together the yogurt, honey, lemon rind and parsley.

5. Put the lettuce leaves onto individual salad plates and arrange the avocado and apricots on top in a sunflower design.

6. Spoon a little of the yogurt mixture over the salad, and sprinkle with sunflower seeds. Pour any remaining yogurt dressing into a small jug and serve separately.

TIME: Preparation takes about 15 minutes.

VARIATIONS: Use segments of ruby grapefruit in place of the apricots.

SERVING IDEAS: Serve as an unusual first course, or as an accompaniment to a chicken or fish dish.

Rice and Nut Salad

This refreshing salad is high in protein from the rice, nuts and beans, so it could be eaten as a vegetarian main course.

SERVES 4

2 tbsps olive oil
2 tbsps lemon juice
Freshly ground sea salt and black pepper
120g/4oz sultanas
60g/2oz currants
275g/10oz cooked brown rice, well drained
90g/3oz blanched almonds, chopped
60g/2oz cashew nuts, chopped
60g/2oz shelled walnuts, chopped
425g/15oz can peach slices in natural juice, drained and chopped
¼ cucumber, cubed
120g/4oz cooked red kidney beans
A few pitted black olives

1. Put the olive oil, lemon juice and salt and pepper into a screw top jar. Shake vigorously, until the mixture has thickened.

2. Put the sultanas and the currants into a small bowl, and cover with boiling water. Allow to stand for 10 minutes, before draining the fruit.

3. Mix together the rice, nuts, soaked fruit, peaches, cucumber, kidney beans and olives in a large mixing bowl.

4. Pour the dressing over the salad, and mix together thoroughly, to ensure all the ingredients are evenly coated.

TIME: Preparation will take about 15 minutes.

PREPARATION: If you would like to create a slightly unusual flavour, soak the sultanas and currants in hot jasmine tea, instead of water.

VARIATIONS: Use a 425g/15oz can apricot halves in natural juice, in place of the can of peaches.

SERVING IDEAS: Serve the salad on a bed of crisp lettuce, or endive, chopped.

Creamy Sweetcorn and Peppers

Sweetcorn is essential to this recipe, but other vegetables can be added, too. Choose your favourites or use what you have to hand.

SERVES 6

60ml/4 tbsps oil
30g/1oz butter
2 medium onions, finely chopped
1 clove garlic, crushed
1 medium green pepper, cut into small dice
6 tomatoes, skinned, seeded and diced
225g/8oz frozen corn kernels
280ml/½ pint chicken or vegetable stock
Pinch salt
60ml/4 tbsps double cream
Pinch of paprika

1. Heat the oil in a large casserole and add the butter. When foaming, add the onions and garlic and cook, stirring frequently, for about 5 minutes or until both are soft and transparent but not browned.

2. Add the green pepper, tomatoes, corn and stock. Bring to the boil over high heat.

3. Reduce the heat, partially cover the casserole and allow to cook slowly for about 10 minutes, or until the corn is tender. Add salt and stir in the cream. Heat through, sprinkle with paprika and serve immediately.

TIME: Preparation takes about 25 minutes. Cooking takes about 10 minutes.

VARIATIONS: Use canned tomatoes, coarsely chopped.

COOK'S TIP: Sweetcorn toughens if cooked at too high a temperature for too long, or if boiled too rapidly.

Buttered Mixed Vegetables

A tasty and colourful dish you can make in no time at all!

SERVES 6

120g/4oz frozen sweetcorn
120g/4oz frozen broad beans
120g/4oz frozen French beans
45g/1½oz butter
Salt and pepper
Chopped parsley

1. Bring water to the boil in a saucepan and, when boiling, add the vegetables. Cook for about 5-8 minutes, drain and leave to dry.

2. Melt the butter in a saucepan and add the vegetables. Heat slowly, tossing or stirring occasionally, until heated through. Add salt and pepper to taste and stir in the parsley. Serve immediately.

TIME: Preparation takes about 10 minutes, cooking takes 5-8 minutes.

VARIATIONS: The recipe can be made with just corn and broad beans or corn and French beans. Add red or green pepper, or chopped onion for flavour variation.

Strawberry Cloud

It takes no time at all to make this delightful summer dessert.

SERVES 4-6

450g/1lb strawberries
1 × 275g/10oz pack silken tofu
Juice of ½ lemon
2 tbsps soft brown sugar
Few drops vanilla essence

1. Wash and hull the strawberries. Leave a few on one side to decorate.

2. Drain the tofu and put into the liquidiser together with the strawberries, lemon juice and sugar.

3. Liqùidise until smooth.

4. Add vanilla essence to taste and mix well.

5. Divide the mixture between 4-6 individual serving dishes and decorate with the reserved strawberries.

6. Chill until required.

TIME: Preparation takes 5-8 minutes.

SERVING IDEAS: For a special occasion, pipe whipped cream around the edges of the serving dishes.

VARIATIONS: Other fruits such as apples or peaches may be used instead but they will not produce such a colourful dessert.

COOK'S TIP: Substitute cream cheese for tofu if wished and add lemon juice to taste.

ALMOND-STUFFED FIGS

Fresh figs are now easily available from most major supermarkets and good greengrocers. When ripe, they go a luscious purple black and are soft to the touch.

SERVES 4

4 large ripe figs
45g/4 tbsps ground almonds
2 tbsps orange juice
2 tbsps finely chopped dried apricots
60ml/4 tbsps natural yogurt
Finely grated rind ½ orange
Wedges of figs, and mint or strawberry leaves for decoration

1. Cut each fig into quarters using a sharp knife, taking care not to cut right down through the base.

2. Ease the four sections of each fig outward to form a flower shape.

3. Put the ground almonds, orange juice and chopped apricots into a small bowl and mix together thoroughly.

4. Divide this mixture into four, and press it into the centre of each fig.

5. For the sauce, mix the yogurt with the orange rind, and thin it down with just a little water, or orange juice.

6. Spoon a small pool of orange yogurt onto each of four plates, and sit a stuffed fig into the centre of each pool. Decorate with the additional wedges of fig, and the mint or strawberry leaves.

TIME: Preparation takes approximately 20 minutes.

VARIATIONS: Use peach halves instead of the figs in this recipe.

WATCHPOINT: Do not add too much water or orange juice to the sauce, or it will become too thin.

Cherry Compôte

This makes a special, elegant pudding, but an easy one, too. The contrast of hot brandied cherries and cold ice cream or whipped cream is sensational.

SERVES 4-6

675g/1½lbs canned black cherries
2 tbsps sugar
60ml/4 tbsp brandy
Vanilla ice cream or whipped cream

1. Combine the cherry juice with the sugar and heat through to dissolve it. Add the cherries to the juice.

2. Pour the brandy into a separate saucepan. Heat the brandy and ignite with a match. Combine the brandy with the fruit and leave until the flames die down naturally.

3. Spoon the fruit over ice cream or on its own into serving dishes to be topped with whipped cream. Serve immediately.

TIME: Preparation takes about 10 minutes and cooking takes about 10 minutes.

VARIATIONS: If wished, use fresh cherries. Pit, and cook until softened, in advance, then set aside. At serving time, reheat and continue from Step 2.

COOK'S TIP: If using fresh cherries double the amount of sugar used.

Brown Sugar Bananas

Bananas in a rich brown sugar sauce make a delectable dessert.

SERVES 4

4 ripe bananas, peeled
Lemon juice
120g/4oz butter
120g/4oz soft brown sugar, light or dark
Pinch ground cinnamon and nutmeg
140ml/¼ pint orange juice
60ml/4 tbsps white or dark rum
Juice of ½ lemon
140ml/¼ pint whipped cream
2 tbsps chopped pecans

1. Cut the bananas in half lengthwise and sprinkle with lemon juice on all sides.

2. Melt the butter in a large frying pan and add the sugar, cinnamon, nutmeg and orange juice. Stir over gentle heat until the sugar dissolves into a syrup.

3. Add the banana halves and cook gently for about 3 minutes, basting the bananas often with syrup, but not turning them.

4. Once the bananas are heated through, warm the rum in a small saucepan and ignite with a match. Pour the flaming rum over the bananas and shake the pan gently until the flames die down naturally. Place 2 banana halves on each serving plate and top with some of the whipped cream. Sprinkle with pecans and serve immediately.

TIME: Preparation takes about 15 minutes and cooking takes about 5 minutes for the sugar and butter syrup and 3-4 minutes for the bananas.

SERVING IDEAS: The bananas may be served with vanilla ice cream instead of whipped cream, if wished.

COOK'S TIP: Sprinkling the cut surfaces of the banana with lemon juice keeps them from turning brown and also offsets the sweetness of the sauce.

CRÊPES

These tasty pancakes are delicious with both sweet and tangy sauces.

MAKES 10-12 PANCAKES

120g/4oz plain flour
Pinch salt
1 egg
280ml/½ pint milk
1 tsp vegetable oil
Juice and zested rind of a lemon and orange

1. Sieve the flour and the salt into a large bowl and make a well in the centre.

2. Put the egg and the milk into a jug and beat well.

3. Gradually pour the egg and milk mixture into the centre of the bowl and mix it in gently, stirring and drawing in the flour from the sides, until all has been incorporated. Beat to ensure even mixing.

4. Heat a little oil in a small frying pan, and pour in enough batter to make a thin pancake.

5. Quickly tilt and rotate the frying pan so that the batter coats the bottom of it evenly.

6. Cook the pancake over a moderate heat until the underside has turned brown and the top has set.

7. Carefully turn the pancake over and brown the other side in the same way.

8. Turn each pancake out onto greaseproof paper and keep them warm until required.

9. Serve the pancakes hot with freshly squeezed orange and lemon juice and decorate with the zested citrus rind.

TIME: Preparation takes approximately 10 minutes, cooking takes about 20 minutes for all the pancakes.

WATCHPOINT: Do not overheat your frying pan or the base of the pancake will burn before the top has set. Also, do not attempt to turn the pancake until the underside is properly cooked.

TO FREEZE: Make the pancakes in greater quantities than this recipe, and freeze, interleaved with greaseproof paper, until required.

Sweet Almond Pudding

A delicious variation on a traditional pudding; ground rice was never like this at school!

SERVES 4

180g/6oz blanched almonds
430ml/¾ pint water
180g/6oz sugar
3 tbsps ground rice
140ml/¼ pint milk

1. Blend the blanched almonds and the water in a liquidiser or food processor, until the almonds are well chopped.

2. Put the almond liquid into a medium-sized saucepan and bring this mixture to the boil over a gentle heat.

3. Add the sugar and stir until it has completely dissolved.

4. Blend together the rice and the milk in a jug.

5. Add the rice mixture slowly to the simmering sugar and almond mixture, stirring continuously, until the pudding thickens.

6. Remove the rice pudding from the heat and pour into individual serving dishes.

TIME: Preparation takes about 5 minutes, and cooking takes 6-7 minutes.

VARIATIONS: Lightly toast some flaked or chopped almonds and sprinkle these over the top of the pudding to serve.

SERVING IDEAS: Serve this pudding cold with fresh or stewed fruit.

Oatlet Cookies

A delicious mix of oats, seeds and syrup make these cookies extra special.

MAKES 10 COOKIES

120g/4oz porridge oats
120g/4oz plain flour
90g/3oz sunflower seeds
30g/1oz sesame seeds
½ tsp mixed spice
120g/4oz margarine
1 tbsp brown sugar
1 tsp golden syrup or molasses
½ tsp baking powder
1 tbsp boiling water
225g/8oz chocolate drops

1. Mix the oats, flour, sunflower seeds, sesame seeds and spice together.

2. Melt the margarine, sugar and golden syrup or molasses over a gentle heat.

3. Add the baking powder and water to the syrup mixture and stir well.

4. Pour over dry ingredients and mix.

5. Place spoonfuls of the mixture, well apart, onto a greased baking tray and bake for 10 minutes at 190°C/375°F/Gas Mark 5.

6. Allow to cool on the tray.

7. Melt the chocolate drops in a bowl over hot water and place teaspoonsful of the melted chocolate on top of the cookies. Leave to set. Store in an airtight tin.

TIME: Preparation takes 15 minutes, cooking takes 10 minutes.

VARIATIONS: Ground ginger can be used in place of the mixed spice.

COOK'S TIP: A block of chocolate may be used in place of the chocolate drops.

Shortbread Biscuits

Sandwich these biscuits together with raspberry jam for children's birthday parties.

MAKES ABOUT 18

150g/5oz plain flour
75g/2½oz light muscovado sugar, finely ground
120g/4oz soft margarine
½ tsp vanilla essence

1. Sieve the flour and sugar together and rub in the margarine.

2. Add the vanilla essence and bind the mixture together.

3. Form into small balls and place on a baking tray a few inches apart.

4. With the back of a fork, press the balls down making a criss-cross pattern.

5. Bake at 190°C/375°F/Gas Mark 5 for about 10-15 minutes until golden brown in colour.

6. Cool on a wire rack.

TIME: Preparation takes 10 minutes, cooking takes 10-15 minutes.

VARIATIONS: Add a tablespoon of currants to make fruit biscuits. Omit the vanilla essence and substitute almond essence to make almond biscuits.

COOK'S TIP: Store these biscuits in an airtight container.

YOGURT SCONES

These scones make a delicious alternative to the more usual plain scones.

MAKES 10 SCONES

60g/2oz butter
225g/8oz wholemeal self-raising flour
30g/1oz demerara sugar
60g/2oz raisins
Natural yogurt to mix

1. Rub the butter into the flour and sugar.

2. Add the raisins and mix well.

3. Slowly stir in enough yogurt to mix to a fairly stiff dough.

4. Turn the mixture onto a floured board and knead lightly.

5. Roll out the dough to about 2cm/¾-inch thick and cut into 5cm/2-inch rounds.

6. Place on a lightly greased baking tray and bake, near the top of the oven, at 220°C/425°F/Gas Mark 7 for 14-16 minutes.

7. Remove from the tray and cool on a wire rack. Serve warm.

TIME: Preparation takes 10 minutes, cooking takes 14-16 minutes.

VARIATIONS: Use chopped dried apricots instead of raisins.

SERVING IDEAS: Serve with jam and cream.

Index